# FATHER
# GOD

DEREK PRINCE

# FATHER GOD

DEREK PRINCE

DEREK PRINCE MINISTRIES
WWW.DEREKPRINCE.COM

# FATHER GOD
By Derek Prince

© 2015 Derek Prince Ministries–International
This edition published by Derek Prince Ministries-UK 2015

ISBN 978-1-78263-307-5
ePub 978-1-78263-308-2
Kindle 978-1-78263-309-9
Product code B121EN3

Derek Prince Ministries
www.derekprince.com

# Contents

# FOREWORD

# FATHER GOD

Do you know God as your Father? This is the profound question Derek Prince addresses in *Father God*, the powerful message you are about to read.

Far from being provocative or critical in any way, the question really comes as an invitation from Derek. In the early pages of this work, you will discover his own deeply personal encounter with Abba, Father.

For Derek, the experience of coming to know God as his Father arose unexpectedly and dramatically out of his own personal need. Very possibly, as you turn these pages, the realization may hit you that you face a situation very similar to Derek's. If that is true, you will be wonderfully encouraged by the message communicated here. Derek's own testimony—totally grounded in a biblical presentation—affirms a marvelous truth: **you and I can experience the Fatherhood of God for ourselves.** That reality will stir the hearts of all who long for the life-changing experience of knowing God as Abba, Father.

You need to be aware of one other factor as you read this message. Derek's overriding hope and belief in presenting this teaching was that it might have its greatest impact upon future generations of believers. His passion comes across loud and clear in these pages. Here is how he so pointedly expressed it:

> *"In view of the fatherless generations all around us, we recognize that no one is ever going to be satisfied until they have a father. It is our privilege to tell them there is a Father who loves them. There is a Father who is waiting for them, who will not condemn them, who will not criticize them, who will not point out all their faults and failings. He is just waiting. I believe if we could get that message across to the fatherless generations all around us, many of them would run into their Father's arms. That is what they are longing for."*

As you read these words, a deep longing may rise in your own heart for the connection Derek has described here. That stirring you sense may in itself be the strongest indication that this teaching is for you—and that a life-changing event of your own is awaiting you in these pages. What Derek conveys here is absolutely true: You can have your very own personal encounter with Father God. If that happens, it will fulfill our greatest hope (and Derek's as well) in presenting this teaching.

There is a wonderful little chorus called *Father God, I Give All Thanks*. It was a personal favorite of one of Derek Prince's dear, departed friends— Pastor Bill Cooper from Naples, Florida. In his rich baritone voice, Bill would regularly close his church services in Naples with a rendition of this song, written by another well-known minister, Pastor Jack Hayford. The simple words of the chorus go like this:

> *Father God,*
> *I give all thanks and praise to Thee.*
> *Father God,*
> *My hands I humbly raise to Thee.*
> *For Your mighty power and love*
> *Amazes me, amazes me—*
> *And I stand in awe and worship, Father God.*

Maybe before you even turn the next page of this booklet, you might want to lift those words to the Lord in faith. Let them express your thanks in advance for the wonderful truths you are about to receive.

It is our hope and prayer that by reading *Father God*, your heart will be filled to overflowing. May you truly experience a fresh revelation of God as your Father, enabling you—in a brand new way—to "...stand in awe and worship Father God."

— The International Publishing Team of
   Derek Prince Ministries

# INTRODUCTION

# A PROCLAMATION

If someone were to ask you if you truly know your father, how would you respond? That important issue is the main subject of this booklet. It is a topic that has an impact upon each of us—every day of our lives. The theme of this message is "knowing your father"—specifically, *Knowing God as Your Father.*

In this introduction, I would like to begin our exploration of this topic with a proclamation. Our declaration is taken from the First Epistle of John, chapter 3, verses 1, 2 and 3. I invite you to join me in proclaiming this passage out loud (if you are in a place where you can do so):

*Behold what manner of love the Father has bestowed on us, that we should be called children of God! [Indeed, we are !] Therefore the world does not know us, because it did not know Him. Beloved, now we are children of God; and it has not yet been revealed what we shall be, but we know that when He is revealed, we shall be like Him, for we shall see Him as He is.*

*And everyone who has this hope in Him purifies himself, just as He is pure.*

In this booklet I want to examine what it really means to know God as your Father. When Jesus taught us *The Lord's Prayer*, He instructed us to begin with the words, "Our Father." By virtue of Jesus' instruction we all have the right language to use, and it is correct. But here is the question that arises: Do we all have the experience? Or is that phrase, "Our Father," just a set of familiar religious words to us?

## Two Main Elements

*Do I truly know God as my Father?* The reality of our experience of God as our Father is vitally important to us. To help us address this matter, I would like to begin with a passage familiar to most Christians. In John 14:6, Jesus says these words:

*"I am the way, the truth, and the life. No one comes to the Father except through Me."*

In that statement there are two key elements:
1) the way, and 2 ) the destination.

What is the way? Clearly, Jesus is the way.

What is the destination? Amazingly, far too many Christians have never even considered that question.

Jesus said, "No one comes to the Father except through Me." Jesus is the way. But *the Father* is the destination.

Through many years of experience and observation, I am aware that multitudes of Christians are "on the way." However they have never truly arrived at their destination. They have never come to know God personally *as a Father*. So they continue "on the way"—they live good lives and they receive many blessings. But they have missed the real point of the reason Jesus came. He came to bring us to the Father.

That is the important issue we will settle and apply personally in this booklet.

# CHAPTER ONE

# It Happened To Me

When it comes to discovering the destination —coming to the Father—I can say that it happened to me. Please allow me to illustrate from personal experience this important distinction between being "on the way" and arriving at the destination—coming to know God as my Father.

I was rather dramatically saved in the middle of the night in an Army barrack room during World War II. My salvation experience took place in the year 1941, in the seaside town of Scarborough in Yorkshire, England. I didn't know anything about the doctrine of salvation. I simply had the experience. (I later discovered that there were people who had the doctrine but didn't have the experience. Frankly, if I had to choose, I would rather have the experience than the doctrine. The good news is that you can have both! Never be content with the doctrine without the experience.)

The night I came to know Jesus personally, I experienced salvation—and my life was dramatically and permanently revolutionized. That transformation continued over many years of walking with the Lord. I never became a backslider. Many times I was not what I should have been, but I never turned my back on the Lord. Over those next decades, God blessed me and used me to preach the gospel in over fifty nations. But an experience awaited me that would transform me even more dramatically than all I had yet encountered.

In 1996, there was a wonderful celebration of my fiftieth year in full-time ministry. The event was attended by many friends, associates and family members. After that time of celebration, Ruth and I went on holiday to Hawaii. We had rented a little apartment and intended to go there to rest. What we experienced, however, was far from rest.

Actually, as I look back on the years, it is quite amazing how many times we would go somewhere to rest, but find it impossible to do so. In fact, it became almost a foregone conclusion that, no matter what our intentions were, we wouldn't rest. This particular holiday was no exception. During that time in Hawaii, I ended up having surgery, Ruth struggled with illness, and there were all kinds of disruptions.

Even though there were some impediments, we had come to Hawaii to rest. So each morning we would sit up in bed and pray and worship. We would also take communion together.

## The Skullcap

One morning just after we had finished our time of worship and prayer, we were sitting together in the bed. Right then, something quite unexpected—something very distinct and very physical—began to happen to me. I found that a power was moving in my feet, then in my legs, and then up my body. At the same time, I was aware of what seemed like a long arm stretched out from somewhere over my right ear—trying to force something down on top of my head that I might only describe as a black skullcap.

It was as if I was caught in a conflict between these two powers—one affecting my body, and one pressing down on my head. Ruth later told me that my whole body was gripped by this struggle. She said, "Your color changed to purple." This experience was totally objective—it was not something imaginary or subjective.

For a little while I didn't know what was going to happen next. Then suddenly, the power that was working in my body overpowered the long arm that was trying to force the black skullcap onto my head. The arm was withdrawn—and then something happened. Immediately I knew God as my Father. It became totally natural from that point on for me to say "*Father*" in a way it had never been before.

In processing the experience I just described, it is important for you to understand that up until this point I had possessed the doctrinal knowledge of the fatherhood of God for many years. In fact, I had even recorded a series of three messages entitled *Knowing God as Father*.

I had all the theory, and it was true. It was correct. There was nothing incorrect or insincere about what I believed. But what I didn't have was the experience. I had found the way, and I had been "on the way" a long while. But I had not arrived at the destination.

# Chapter Two

# Coming to Know
# the Father

What I have described from my own experience about being "on the way" for a long while is probably true for many believers—perhaps even for you. That is why it is so vital for us to focus on coming to the destination—coming to know the Father. In a profound way, the experience I had in Hawaii revolutionized my entire life. It especially revolutionized my prayer life.

As you probably know, I am from a British military background. Every male member of my family that I have ever known personally has been an officer in the British Army. Like my relatives, I am a disciplined type of person. In addition, I had been blessed with a very real and dramatic experience of conversion—one which I have never doubted. But the revelation I describe in these pages was one which was totally new to me—to know God as Father.

I thank God for my parents and my grandparents. They were fine people. They had a sense of duty which hardly exists in people today. But as for a sense of knowing anybody as a father—well, that just was not present in our family.

In my family nobody hugged anybody. One of my clearest memories is when, at the age of nine, I was sent off to boarding school. There I was, in my little bowler hat—embarrassed to kiss my mother goodbye in public. I don't think my father ever took me on his knee. There just wasn't that kind of relationship in our family. They were moral people, good people, dutiful people. But there was a whole dimension of love and intimacy and freedom which we never knew.

Like many Christians, when I came into the baptism in the Holy Spirit I experienced an outpouring of new freedom and power. But never had I experienced a breakthrough like the one in that little apartment in Hawaii. After that skullcap was removed, immediately I knew God as my Father.

## A Dark Force

I have theories about the skullcap mentioned earlier. These theories have come from my years of ministering in the realm of spiritual warfare. I have discovered, in ministering to countless people for healing and deliverance, that our early years are often the most decisive in our overall spiritual experience.

In my case, although I was British, I was actually born in Bangalore, India, and lived there for the first five years of my childhood.

India is a nation of three million gods, and I think some of the gods of India followed after me for many years. In fact, many times throughout my life, I was aware of the presence of some dark force.

Even though I was saved, baptized in the Holy Spirit, speaking in tongues, praying for people, and seeing the sick healed, I always seemed to sense that somewhere in the background something dark was hovering over me. I believe it was an Indian god, and I believe I know its name. (I'm not going to repeat it here because the Bible tells us not to use the names of foreign gods.)

Deuteronomy 12:3 says, "You shall cut down the carved images of their gods and destroy their names from that place." So, without revealing its name, I believe this Indian god followed me up through my life—through more than fifty years of Christian ministry. Up until the breakthrough that I experienced in Hawaii, the power of that dark presence had never been totally vanquished.

As I said earlier, I have seen from my ministry in spiritual warfare (which has been extensive) that the events that happen early in our lives are sometimes the most decisive. Often they are the most difficult to deal with—even if they happened to us while we were still in our mother's womb, before we were actually born. It takes the work of the Holy Spirit to uncover what is hidden and show us how to deal with those issues. This may be the case for you. This booklet may help to bring you—not only into a knowledge of God as your Father—but into a new level of spiritual freedom as well.

# CHAPTER THREE

# Jesus—The Ultimate Messenger

As we begin this section, let me just issue a disclaimer. I am not a psychologist, nor am I a psychiatrist. I am just a preacher. But since my breakthrough in Hawaii, there has been a profound, ongoing change in my spiritual experience. My purpose here is to give you a scriptural basis which will enable you to come into the same kind of relationship with God the Father. What I share will not just be based on subjective personal experience. It will be grounded solidly in the Word of God.

Let's begin by reading in Hebrews chapter 1, verses 1 and 2. This passage of Scripture says:

*God, who at various times and in different ways spoke in time past to the fathers by the prophets, has in these last days spoken to us by His Son* [In my Bible the word "His" is in italics, which means it's not there in the original text], *whom He has appointed heir of all things, through whom also He made the worlds* [or the ages]; . . .

This passage from Hebrews is comparing two different ways in which God speaks. He speaks by the prophets. But in a totally different way, He speaks by His Son. It is not a difference of *persons*—it is a difference of *ways*. I like Andrew Murray's translation: "*spoken to us sonwise.*" In speaking to us in the second way, God was using a different kind of approach.

The prophets could reveal God's message. But when God wanted to reveal Himself as Father, there was only one person in the universe who could do that. That was the Son. For this very reason, the Son came—not only to complete and fulfill the message of the prophets, but also to present a revelation that no prophet could ever convey. Jesus came to bring the revelation of the Father.

## Who Best Reveals the Father?

In chapter 17 of the book of John, we have what is known as the "high priestly prayer of Jesus." The night before His crucifixion, Jesus prayed this prayer to the Father on behalf of His disciples, who were with Him there in the Upper Room. In one part of this prayer—verse 6 of John 17—Jesus says;

*"I have manifested Your name to the men* [His

disciples] *whom You have given me out of the world. They were Yours, You gave them to Me, and they have kept Your Word."*

I want to put forth some questions for you regarding two aspects of this verse. First of all, what name had Jesus manifested? Remember, for about fourteen centuries the Jewish people had been familiar with the name *Jehovah* or *Yahweh*. This was the sacred name of God which was never pronounced—only written—by the Jewish people. They had known that name. It was not something new to them.

But what was the name which Jesus manifested to His disciples? When you read the "high priestly prayer" you will find the name. What is it? It is "Father." This name occurs six times in John 17. Jesus came to manifest the name of the Father. The word *manifest* is important, because He didn't just come to *talk* about the name "Father." He came to *demonstrate* it.

Secondly, how did Jesus demonstrate the reality of the Father to His disciples? By living like a Son of God. Jesus was never frightened, never perplexed, never in despair. He never failed to know what to do. Why? Because the Father was always with Him.

The disciples saw in the way Jesus lived a totally different kind of life. They were familiar with the prophets. They were familiar with Moses. They were familiar with men who had done tremendous signs and wonders and spoken mighty words. But here was a Man who lived *knowing* that He had a Father in heaven.

Jesus, by His whole life from beginning to end, manifested the name "Father." That is why He came. That is why God sent Him—because only a Son could reveal the Father. The prophets could speak about God and teach about God, but they could not reveal Him. Nor could they manifest Him. Only the Son could reveal the Father.

## Only the Son

In Matthew 11:27, Jesus says this about His relationship to the Father:

> *"All things have been delivered to Me by My Father, and no one knows the Son except the Father. Nor does anyone know the Father except the Son, and the one to whom the Son wills to reveal Him."*

This is an extraordinary statement; "No one knows the Son but the Father, and no one knows the Father but the Son, *and the one to whom the Son wills to reveal the Father."*

Based on this verse, I want to state very clearly that I cannot reveal the Father to you—nor can any preacher do so. There is only one person who can reveal the Father—and that is the Son.

If you are to know the Father it must be by the revelation of the Son. There is no other way.

## Timeless Words of Comfort

I love these well-known words in the next three verses of Matthew 11. They have comforted people over many generations.

*"Come to Me, all you who labor and are heavy laden, and I will give you rest."* (verse 28)

Oh, those words in Greek are so vivid! All you who are carrying burdens. Who are struggling. Who find it hard going. Who sometimes wonder if you will ever make it through. Jesus says, "Come to Me…and I will give you rest."

*"Take My yoke upon you and learn from Me, for I am gentle and lowly in heart, and you will find rest for your souls. For My yoke is easy and My burden is light."* (verses 29-30)

For Jesus, what was His yoke and His burden? It was to do the Father's will. It was His relationship with the Father. He said, "If you're struggling, if you're perplexed, if you're anxious, if you're frustrated, if you're not satisfied with the way your life is going, come to Me. I can reveal the Father to you, and that will be a life-changing revelation. It will give you a new sense of belonging. It will bring you into true rest."

Let me ask you: are you really enjoying rest? I think you would agree that there is not much rest in our contemporary culture. If you are looking there for rest, you will look in vain. Do you know what rest is? Do you know what it is to relax?

There is only one place you can truly find rest—in the bosom of the Father. Jesus will reveal Him to you. I can't do it. I can tell you about it. I can pray for you. But only Jesus can reveal the Father and bring you into His rest

# CHAPTER FOUR

# RESULTS OF KNOWING THE FATHER

In an earlier chapter I shared the transforming experience I had when Ruth and I were in Hawaii. The shadow of darkness that had followed me all my life was removed once and for all by the power of the Holy Spirit. Suddenly, I knew God as my Father in a way I never had experienced before. For fifty years I had the right doctrine but didn't realize I had never had the experience—until that breakthrough!

In the last few chapters we have added an examination of the Scriptures to undergird the experience I described. Through the passages covered in those chapters, we have discovered an objective, doctrinal basis on which you, too, can ask Jesus Christ to reveal the Father. As we have seen, only the Son can reveal the Father. And that is what He intends to do for you.

## Four Important Benefits

Having a close, intimate relationship with the Father has brought wonderful blessings to my life. Time and space do not permit me to share all of those blessings. For our purposes here, I want to highlight what I consider to be four important results that come from knowing the Father.

### 1. Personal Identity

When you come to know the Father, you come to know who you really are. Throughout the Bible, every person is identified by his father or her father. It may seem tedious to read the genealogies—"and so-and-so was the father of so-and-so, the son of so-and-so," etc. But there is a purpose behind these records. The element which gives a person identity is having and knowing a father.

Even in our English language today, though much has changed, many surnames reflect this truth. They are based upon the names of the father—like Williamson, or Johnson, or Thompson. All that is meant by these names is "the son or daughter of William," "the son or daughter of John," "the son or daughter of Thomas."

All around us, we have had what is basically an identity-less generation—an entire generation of young adults who have no sense of identity. Originally they were called *Generation X*. Then they were called *Generation Y*. What does *X* and *Y* stand for? The unknown quantity. Many from that generation simply do not know who they are.

I believe that if we could transfer to this and other future generations the knowledge of their true identity, there would be a tremendous response. There are millions of young people just milling around—lost, confused, perplexed— because they don't know the Father. I don't believe anything of substance will take place for them until they come to know the Father.

You may be reading these words right now, saying to yourself: "This applies to me." You may feel that you don't really know who you are. You may feel as if you are a kind of faceless person—a rootless person who doesn't count anywhere. If that is true for you, the reason it is true is because you don't have a real identity. You may have an identity that you can put on—like clothes, or like makeup. But you know it is not your true, genuine identity.

If you are longing to know your true identity, you can. You will find your identity as you come to know God as your Father.

## 2. A Home in Heaven

The second benefit you have when you know the Father is a home in heaven. From the day I was saved, I always believed that if I continued in the faith—faithfully serving God—I would end up in heaven. I knew heaven was my destination. However, I had never really thought about heaven as my home until I came to know the Father.

You see, what makes a home a home is a father. After I had the experience in Hawaii I said to my wife, "Ruth, I don't care whether you put up a tombstone over me after I die or not. But if you do put up a tombstone, I want you to put just two words on it: "GONE HOME."

I am reminded of a precious Hawaiian sister we knew. She was a dear friend who had served the Lord faithfully for many years. We had some interaction with this friend during the time Ruth and I were in Hawaii. When we last saw her, she was dying of cancer. The fellowship of believers to which she belonged made sure there was always someone by her bed with her—every hour of every day. Quite often she would remark, "You know, I've never seen an angel. I'd love to see an angel." On the day that she passed away, as she was about to die, she sat up in bed, stretched out her hands, and said "I see them! I see the angels!" The next moment she was gone. The angels had come to take her home.

Let's focus for a moment on this aspect of going home to heaven. To begin that focus let me ask you a question: How do you expect to go home?

The 16th chapter of Luke contains the story of a beggar who was lying outside a rich man's door. He was called Lazarus (not the same Lazarus whom Jesus raised from the dead). Day after day, Lazarus lay at the rich man's door, sick and full of sores. But he was a believer. The dogs came and licked his sores in compassion.

In verse 22 of Luke 16, the Bible says,

*"So it was that the beggar died, and was carried by the angels to Abraham's bosom."*

What impressed me in this verse is that it was not just *an* angel—it was *the* angels. I think one strong angel could have easily transported Lazarus' emaciated frame. But God sent an escort of angels to that poor beggar lying in the street.

The story goes on to say of the rich man, "He died, and being in hell he lifted up his eyes…" What a different destiny! I am persuaded that God really wants to send angels to His believing sons and daughters. Why should we go home lonely? Why shouldn't we have an escort? God certainly has enough angels to bring us to our home in heaven.

As a young preacher, I was deeply impressed by the journals of John Wesley. Obviously, Wesley felt it was important the way a believer dies. One day he received a report of a certain Methodist sister who had died. His comment was this: "Did she go in glory or only in peace?"

Which way are you going to go? Only in peace? Or do you believe you are going to have a glorious entry into the Father's mansion, carried there by an escort of angels? It makes a difference when God is your Father. You have a home. You're not a stray. You're not a wanderer. You are on a pathway that is leading home.

### 3. *Total Security*

The third benefit that comes through knowing the Father is total security. In Matthew 10:29, Jesus makes the following observation to his disciples:

*"Are not two sparrows sold for a copper coin? And not one of them falls to the ground apart from your Father's will."*

In this verse, Jesus says that two sparrows are sold for one copper coin. The same account in Luke 12:6-7 tells us that five sparrows are sold for two copper coins. So if you bought four, you apparently got one extra sparrow for free. They were of so little value that you could get five for two copper coins—basically, two pennies. Yet Jesus said, "Not one of them falls to the ground without your Father's will." Then Jesus makes this point in verse 7:

> "Do not fear therefore; you are of more value than many sparrows."

Every now and then you will see a little boy or a little girl held in a father's arms—lifted up, cheek pressed against the father's lapel. There may be chaos all around. Everything may seem to be falling apart. But that little child is not the least bit disturbed. Why? Because he or she is in the father's arms.

That is how God wants us to be—safe in the Father's arms. No matter what storms rage, no matter what evil forces assail us, God wants us to say, "I'm in my Father's arms. I'm content to be a little child."

That longing applies to each of us—no matter how old we are. Even as I have gotten older, I still like to think of myself as being held in my Father's arms.

In John 10:29, Jesus says:

> "My Father, who has given them to Me, is greater than all; and no one is able to snatch them out of My Father's hand."

When you are in the Father's hand, there is nothing that can snatch you away. We are living in times when it is very important to be in the Father's hand. The world around us is not going to get better, believe me. It is going to get darker and fiercer.

Life isn't going to get easier, nor will it get any less dangerous. In fact, it is probably going to get *more* dangerous. With that realization, it is very, very important that you know you are safe in the Father's hand. Jesus said, "My Father is greater than all. There is no one that can snatch you from the Father's hand."

### 4. *True Motivation*

Finally, knowing the Father provides motivation for serving Him. I believe this truth is often neglected among Christians. In John 8:29 Jesus said this about His own relationship with the Father:

> *"And He* [the Father] *who sent Me is with Me. The Father has not left Me alone, for I always do those things that please Him."*

What was the motivation for Jesus' service? Was it success? Was it popularity? Or was it simply to please the Father? Pleasing the Father was Jesus' motive, and I believe that we as Christians urgently need this same motive restored to us. It is so important for the Body of Christ.

Frankly, one of the central problems in the Church today is competition between ministers and ministries. *"Do I have the biggest mailing list? Do the most people attend my meetings? Am I on the most television stations?"*

People think success provides security. It doesn't. In fact, the more successful you are, the more insecure you can be—because you might lose any success you have achieved. Someone else might have a bigger mailing list, or draw a larger crowd, or be on more television stations. Then where will your security be? Security does indeed come out of your motive. "My motive," Jesus said, "is to please My Father."

As we end this chapter I want to recap those four benefits of knowing the Father—because they are so very important for us.

*1. A Sense of Personal Identity*: Knowing the Father helps you come to understand who you really are.

*2. A Sense of Having a Home in Heaven*: Knowing the Father settles the issue of where you will spend eternity. You will be at home with Him.

*3. A Sense of Total Security*: Knowing the Father gives you confidence that nothing and no one can snatch you from His hand.

*4. A Sense of True Motivation*: Knowing the Father gives you the primary goal for all that you do—pleasing Him.

We will cover all four of these benefits once more at the close of this booklet. However, in the chapter that follows I want to enlarge upon the topic raised in point number four—true motivation. I will share some of my own personal testimony in this area of motivation and success. Hopefully, our discussion will help us to discover the power and fulfillment that comes to us when we make it our goal to please the Father in all we do.

# CHAPTER FIVE

# TRUE SUCCESS

In the later years of my life, I have found that this experience of coming to know God as my Father has completely changed my motivation. Even as a child, and as a young boy, I was very success-oriented. It just so happened I was very successful. I was always at the head of the class. As a young lad, I obtained a scholarship to Eton. From Eton I obtained a scholarship to King's College, Cambridge. At King's College, Cambridge, I became the senior student among my peers. At a very early age—age twenty-four—I was elected to a Fellowship. So I know what success is. But success didn't give me security.

In my growing disillusionment I became a "hippie" before my time—actually, before there were any real hippies. When World War II erupted I became a conscientious objector. This step on my part was a pretty difficult decision to make since my father was a colonel, my grandfather was a major general and my uncle was a brigadier in the British Army. For me to be a conscientious objector was certainly not in the family tradition!

As part of the enlistment process I had to go before a tribunal. The vice provost at King's College was the man conducting the tribunal concerning my stance on military service. He asked me, "Are you willing to serve in a non-combatant unit?" I said, "Fine, as long as I don't have to kill people." So that is how I ended up in the Royal Army Medical Corps.

I have to say it was really not the kind of career that suited me. But you see, that is when I got saved. As long as I was walking around Cambridge in my Fellow's gown, strolling across the green, and drinking in the Fellow's lounge, I really didn't need God too much. But all those amenities were stripped away from me when I enlisted in the Army at the lowest possible level.

I became, by a freak of promotion, a "local-acting-unpaid-lance-corporal" (L-A-U-L-C). People who were not familiar with the British army, seeing all those initials and dashes, would often ask me, "What is a 'local-acting-unpaid-lance-corporal?'" I would reply to those people, "It's like being as near as you can be to being a worm without being a worm." But that was the station of life I was in when I got saved. It was then that God radically and totally transformed me.

## The Way Up is Down

I have often said that promotion comes with salvation. Sure enough—contrary to all Army regulations (because I had been a conscientious objector)—I was promoted. Immediately I was assigned to a non-commissioned officer's course.

With my background, it really wasn't a problem for me to stand on parade grounds and shout at people and tell them what to do. In fact, it was second nature to me. I passed the course easily. When I returned from my training I received orders that I was to be promoted to corporal. As I said, "Salvation brings promotion."

The commanding officer was a doctor from Northern Ireland: Col. Dan McVicker. He was the one who sent for me to tell me about my promotion. (If you haven't been in the British Army, there are ways of handling matters you couldn't possibly understand.) But I'll try to explain with the following exchange.

Col. McVicker said to me, "Good morning,

Corporal Prince."

I replied, "Good morning, sir."

He then said, "How's the cooking going?"

Well, that was a totally unexpected question. But when you have been in the army a few months, you learn discretion—you don't commit yourself. So I gave him a non-committal answer.

> I said, "It's seems about the same as usual, sir."
> (Which, in my judgment, was awful.)

> Col. McVicker said, "Didn't you know you're the
> corporal cook of this unit?"

> I said, "No, sir. No one ever told me."

"Well," he said, "we wanted to promote you, but there was no vacancy for corporal except for a cook. So we made you corporal cook."

By the mercy of God I never did any cooking! But it was during that time that I met the Lord—when I was as near to being a worm as you can be without being one.

I still had this inate drive for success—I was very much a success-oriented person. However, I didn't esteem success in the army the way the world did. I certainly didn't expect to be promoted as an officer, though I did expect to succeed in the ministry. Instead, God brought me to a place of almost total despair.

As a pastor, I used to hold meetings in London. Three days a week I would hold meetings at Speaker's Corner, Marble Arch. There we saw people saved, we saw people healed, and we saw people baptized in the Holy Spirit (at a time when that experience was still very rare).

Yet I had this awful problem. *Depression*. There was something deep within me that said, "Others may succeed, but you cannot." So God allowed me to go right down to the bottom. Then He revealed to me that I was deeply troubled by demonic oppression—a spirit of heaviness. When He opened my eyes to that demonic affliction, I called upon the Lord and I was delivered from it. Even so, God had to let me come all the way down before He would lift me up.

## Motives of the Heart

From that point on in my ministry, I went on to become somewhat successful. But success doesn't bring security. As I said, the more successful you are, the more you may be threatened by other people's success.

As much as I would like to believe that this is not a problem in the Body of Christ, I know that it is. I have known too many leaders who had this attitude: "This is my church. I'm the pastor. This is our movement. We're the biggest, etc., etc., etc.!" I am not criticizing the desire to succeed. Most of these leaders are very fine Christians. I am just making the point that success is not the way to security.

Security is actually very simple. In its essence it is knowing God as your Father and making it your aim to please Him. There is no situation in which you cannot be motivated by that desire.

For example, you may be in a traffic jam, late for an appointment. There you are, sitting at the wheel, fuming while you are stuck there in your car—your fists clenched on the steering wheel. You are completely tense. But then you stop and ask yourself, "What am I doing? Am I acting in a way that pleases my Father?" It doesn't matter what your circumstances are. It is your reactions that matter. You are there to please the Father.

We may not have totally mastered the process of pleasing the Father in every situation, but we can get a lot nearer to it than we have in the past. For my part, I want to be governed by this intense desire to please my Father—my heavenly Father. I wouldn't trade that incentive for any other motivation that is in the Body of Christ.

You see, where the followers of Jesus Christ and the leaders in the Body of Christ are motivated that way, there is no room for competition. If each of us is equally set on pleasing the Father, we will never compete with one another. The right motivation contains a deep secret that militates against our tendency toward competition. That secret, powerful motivation comes to us through knowing the Father.

# CHAPTER SIX

## Longing for the Father

As we bring this booklet to a close in this final chapter, let me recapitulate briefly the four benefits that come through knowing the Father.

*First, Personal Identity*. You know who you are because you know who your Father is.

In view of the fatherless generations all around us, we recognize that no one is ever going to be satisfied until they have a father. It is our privilege to tell them there is a Father Who loves them. There is a Father Who is waiting for them, Who will not condemn them, Who will not criticize them, Who will not point out all their faults and failings. He is just waiting. I believe if we could get that message across to the fatherless generations around us, many of them would run into their Father's arms. That is what they are longing for.

But the only way we can communicate this truth is the way Jesus communicated it to His disciples. It is not by preaching, although that can play a part. It is by living as sons and daughters of God. Living in security. Not carrying some heavy load, but trusting Him whose burden is light and whose yoke is easy.

When those who are longing for the Father's love see people like that, they become interested. They will ask you; "What makes you different? Why don't you have furrows in your brow? Why aren't you worried about money? Why aren't you taking sedatives?" Here are your answers to these questions: "I know the Father. He cares for me. He provides for me. My Father feeds the sparrows and He feeds me." That response is not always easy, but it is the goal. It is the solution.

***Second, A Home in Heaven.*** I am looking forward to getting home. I have been a long while on the way—more than five decades—and I have many precious brothers and sisters who are there ahead of me. I'm looking forward to meeting them again.

Death doesn't frighten me. I have to be careful that I don't become almost ambitious for it. I say that carefully because I don't believe my job is finished—and my aim is to finish His work.

Jesus said in John 4:34:

> *"My food is to do the will of Him who sent me, and to finish His work."* (NKJV)

God made that verse very real to me a number of years ago. I went around telling people, "I've got a new diet." They would ask, "What is it?" I would answer, "My food is to do the Father's will and to

finish His work."

The truth is, we have a home in heaven. Heaven has become very real to me. There are some sentimental songs that nobody sings today, but I rather like them.

*Sometimes I grow homesick for Heaven,*
*And the glories I there shall behold;*
*What a joy that shall be when my Savior I see,*
*In that beautiful city of gold.*

Such a song as this may seem corny, but I like it. I used to be very complicated, very intellectual, very profound. Now I am very simple. I have a home in heaven. I have a Father who loves me. I have a Savior who is waiting for me. And I have wonderful brothers and sisters who are there ahead of me!

In many of my messages I have mentioned Ali, the Sudanese Muslim whom I led to the Lord many years ago. I trust by the grace of God he will be there in heaven. I know he will say to me, "Thank you. I'm here because of you."

Will there be anybody in heaven who will say that to you? "Thank you. I'm here because of you." That is a very meaningful consideration.

*Third, Total Security.* I believe we have dealt with this benefit pretty thoroughly, but some of what we have already seen is worth repeating. You are in the Father's arms. You are held by Him—and no one

can snatch you out of the Father's hand! There is no power in the universe that can do that!

Jesus said in John 10:29, "My Father, who has given them to Me, is greater than all, and no one is able to snatch them out of My Father's hand". We have the greatest Father! The most wonderful Father! A God who is above all other gods. Whose hands are on the corners of the universe. He created the angels and the stars, and He is worshiped by millions and millions of glorious beings in heaven. Even so, He is waiting for little creations like you and me to turn up. Isn't that marvelous?

***Fourth, True Motivation.*** As I have said throughout this message, knowing the Father has made a great difference in my life. Especially, it has provided me with true motivation for service. I'm not out to build the biggest ministry or be the greatest minister. I am out to please my Father.

There are always situations where there is not much you can do. You may be sitting in a doctor's waiting room. You're running late, the doctor is keeping you waiting—and the magazines are pretty boring. What are you going to do? You can please your Father by your attitude—by your response. There is never a situation in which that motivation to please the Father does not apply, if we can successfully cultivate it.

## Come To Your Father

Do you long to know the Father? I believe that you can.

I have said clearly and plainly that I cannot reveal the Father to you. The only one who can do that is Jesus. But if you seek Jesus sincerely and humbly on the basis of His Word, I believe—in His own way and time—He will reveal the Father to you. I want to give you an opportunity to respond right now, asking for this experience in your life.

I know what happened to me, but I can't say exactly what will happen for you. However, if you have a longing that has been stirring in your heart to know God as your Father, why don't you rise out of your seat wherever you are right now? If you can find a place to kneel, simply kneel before the Father and just tell Him:

> *"Father, I want to know You. I thank You for Jesus. He is my Savior. He has changed my life. I know I belong to You. But Father, I want to know You. I'm on the way, but I want to come to the destination."*

I can't guarantee what will take place for you. I don't know what will happen. But I know the Lord has His eye on you right now. If there is a genuine hunger in your heart, Jesus promised, "Blessed are those who hunger and thirst for righteousness, for they shall be filled" (Matthew 5:7). If you are hungry and thirsty right now, Jesus has promised you will be filled.

Here is my invitation to you. If you are hungry and thirsty to know the Father, tell Him so. Go to Him. Wait for Him. Cry out to Him. He is waiting to hear what you long to say to Him.

Let me pray for you as we end this booklet.

*"Father, please show Yourself to the one who is calling to You. Lord Jesus, hear this dear one's cry—and reveal the Father as only You can do. Amen."*

# About the Author

Derek Prince (1915–2003) was born in India of British parents. Educated as a scholar of Greek and Latin at Eton College and Cambridge University, England, he held a Fellowship in Ancient and Modern Philosophy at King's College. He also studied several modern languages, including Hebrew and Aramaic, at Cambridge University and the Hebrew University in Jerusalem.

While serving with the British army in World War II, he began to study the Bible and experienced a life-changing encounter with Jesus Christ. Out of this encounter he formed two conclusions: first, that Jesus Christ is alive; second, that the Bible is a true, relevant, up-to-date book. These conclusions altered the whole course of his life, which he then devoted to studying and teaching the Bible.

Derek's main gift of explaining the Bible and its teaching in a clear and simple way has helped build a foundation of faith in millions of lives. His non-denominational, non-sectarian approach has made his teaching equally relevant and helpful to people from all racial and religious backgrounds.

He is the author of over 50 books, 600 audio and 100 video teachings, many of which have been translated and published in more than 100 languages. His daily radio broadcast is translated into Arabic, Chinese (Amoy, Cantonese, Mandarin, Shanghainese, Swatow), Croatian,

German, Malagasy, Mongolian, Russian, Samoan, Spanish and Tongan. The radio program continues to touch lives around the world.

Derek Prince Ministries persists in reaching out to believers in over 140 countries with Derek's teachings, fulfilling the mandate to keep on "until Jesus returns." This is effected through the outreaches of more than 45 Derek Prince offices around the world, including primary work in Australia, Canada, China, France, Germany, the Netherlands, New Zealand, Norway, Russia, South Africa, Switzerland, the United Kingdom and the United States. For current information about these and other worldwide locations, visit www.derekprince.com.

# Books by Derek Prince

Appointment in Jerusalem
At the End of Time *
Authority and Power of God's
    Word *
Be Perfect
Blessing or Curse: You Can
    Choose
Bought With Blood
By Grace Alone
Called to Conquer
Choice of a Partner, The
Complete Salvation
Declaring God's Word
Derek Prince—A Biography
by Stephen Mansfield
Derek Prince: On Experiencing
    God's Power
Destiny Of Israel and The
    Church, The
Divine Exchange, The
Doctrine of Baptisms, The *
Does Your Tongue Need
    Healing?
End of Life's Journey, The
Entering the Presence of God
Expelling Demons
Explaining Blessings and
    Curses
Extravagant Love
Faith and Works *
Faith to Live By
Fasting

Final Judgment *
First Mile, The
Foundational Truths For
    Christian Living
Founded On the Rock *
Gifts of the Spirit, The
God Is a Matchmaker
God's Medicine Bottle
God's Plan for Your Money
God's Remedy for Rejection
God's Will for Your Life
God's Word Heals
Grace of Yielding, The
Harvest Just Ahead, The
Holy Spirit in You, The
How to Fast Successfully
Husbands and Fathers
I Forgive You
Immersion in The Spirit *
Judging
Keys to Successful Living
Key to the Middle East
Laying the Foundations Series*
Life's Bitter Pool
Life Changing Spiritual Power
Living As Salt and Light
Lucifer Exposed
Marriage Covenant, The
Orphans, Widows, the Poor
    and Oppressed
Our Debt to Israel
Pages from My Life's Book

Partners for Life
Philosophy, the Bible and
    the Supernatural
Power in the Name
Power of the Sacrifice, The
Prayers and Proclamations
Praying for the Government
Promise of Provision, The
Prophetic Guide to the End
    Times
Protection from Deception
Pulling Down Strongholds
Receiving God's Best
Rediscovering God's Church
Resurrection of the Body *
Rules of Engagement
Secrets of a Prayer Warrior
Self-Study Bible Course
    (revised and expanded)
Set Apart For God
Shaping History Through
    Prayer and Fasting
Spiritual Warfare
Surviving the Last Days
Thanksgiving, Praise and
    Worship
They Shall Expel Demons
Through Repentance to Faith *
Through the Psalms with
    Derek Prince
Transmitting God's Power *
The Two Harvests
Three Messages For Israel
Ultimate Security
War in Heaven
Where Wisdom Begins
Who Is the Holy Spirit?
Will You Intercede?
You Matter to God
You Shall Receive Power

# Derek Prince Offices Worldwide

**DPM–Asia/Pacific**
38 Hawdon Street, Sydenham
Christchurch 8023,
New Zealand
T: + 64 3 366 4443
E: admin@dpm.co.nz
W: www.dpm.co.nz and
www.derekprince.in

**DPM–Australia**
Unit 21/317-321
Woodpark Road, Smithfield
New South Wales 2165,
Australia
T: + 612 9604 0670
E: enquiries@derekprince.com.au
W: www.derekprince.com.au

**DPM–Canada**
P. O. Box 8354 Halifax,
Nova Scotia B3K 5M1,
Canada
T: + 1 902 443 9577
E: enquiries.dpm@eastlink.ca
W: www.derekprince.org

**DPM–France**
B.P. 31, Route d'Oupia,
34210 Olonzac,
France
T: + 33 468 913872
E: info@derekprince.fr
W: www.derekprince.fr

**DPM–Germany**
Schwarzauer Str. 56
D-83308 Trostberg,
Germany
T: + 49 8621 64146
E: IBL.de@t-online.de
W: www.ibl-dpm.net

**DPM–Nederland**
Postbus 326
7100 VB
Winterswijk
Phone: (+31) 251-255044
E: info@dpmnederland.nl
W: www.derekprince.nl

**DPM–NORWAY**
P. O. Box 129
Lodderfjord
N-5881, Bergen,
Norway
T: +47 928 39855
E: sverre@derekprince.no
W: www.derekprince.no

**Derek Prince Publications Pte. Ltd.**
P. O. Box 2046 ,
Robinson Road Post Office
Singapore 904046
T: + 65 6392 1812
E: dpmchina@singnet.com.sg
English web: www.dpmchina.org
Chinese web: www.ygmweb.org

**DPM–South Africa**
P. O. Box 33367
Glenstantia 0010 Pretoria
South Africa
T: +27 12 348 9537
E: enquiries@derekprince.co.za
W: www.derekprince.co.za

**DPM–Switzerland**
Alpenblick 8
CH-8934 Knonau
Switzerland
T: + 41(0) 44 768 25 06
E: dpm-ch@ibl-dpm.net
W: www.ibl-dpm.net

**DPM–UK**
Kingsfield, Hadrian Way
Baldock SG7 6AN
UK
T: + 44 (0) 1462 492100
E: enquiries@dpmuk.org
W: www.dpmuk.org

**DPM–USA**
P. O. Box 19501
Charlotte NC 28219,
USA
T: + 1 704 357 3556
E: ContactUs@derekprince.org
W: www.derekprince.org

CPSIA information can be obtained
at www.ICGtesting.com
Printed in the USA
BVHW070634070222
628205BV00006B/757

9 781782 633075